PUBLISHING

Speaking in Sentences

Oral language activities to take the struggle out of literacy

Book 1

Ages 6–10

Jenny Pyatt

Title:	Speaking in Sentences Book 1 (Ages 6-10)
Author:	Jenny Pyatt
Editor:	Tanya Tremewan
Design/Layout:	Michelle Peacock
Book Code:	PB00049
ISBN:	978-1-908735-33-1
Published:	2012
Publisher:	TTS Group Ltd Park Lane Business Park Kirkby-in-Ashfield Notts, NG17 9GU Tel: 0800 318 686 Fax: 0800 137 525
Website:	www.tts-shopping.com

About the author:

Jenny Pyatt has a background of 27 years in teaching pupils from Years 1–8. Her strong interest in helping those for whom English is a second language stemmed from teaching experiences in East and South Auckland, New Zealand.

Now semi-retired and living on a lifestyle block in Hawke's Bay, Jenny spends her time writing, raising calves and tending a four-acre garden.

Contents

Introduction 4

Curriculum links 5

Part 1: Diagnostic tools 6

Language sample 6
Oral language sentences 8
Opposites 10
Plurals 10
Vocabulary 11
Assessment – summary and analysis 12

Part 2: Fun, quick and handy activities 13

Impromptu speeches 13
Story starters 16
Re-telling stories 17
Telephone conversations 17
Hide the object 17
Describing in the negative 17
Practising irregular past tense 18
Expanding vocabulary – positives and negatives 18
I spy 18
Introducing and interviewing a speaker 19
Self-access resources 20

Part 3: Comprehension and related activities 21

Activity One: The story of Pete the Pirate 22
Activity Two: The story of the winding river 23
Activity Three: The story of the horse that got away 24
Activity Four: The story of the ball that rolled and rolled 25
Activity Five: The story of Samantha the Spider 26
Activity Six: The story of Andy the Astronaut 27
Activity Seven: Conversation – what would you like? 29
Activity Eight: Fill the gaps – how often? 30

Part 4: Using pronouns 32

Activity One: Action book 33
Activity Two: *He* and *she* card game 33
Activity Three: *He* and *she* action pictures 36
Activity Four: *He, she, it* and *they* action pictures 37
Activity Five: Sentence completion with *his, her* and *their* 38
Activity Six: Story completion with *his, her* and *they* 39
Activity Seven: Conversation – what can you see? 40

Part 5: Sequence stories 41

Activity One: Andy the Astronaut's space trip 42
Activity Two: Building a story from pictures 43
Activity Three: The life cycle of a frog 44
Activity Four: The life cycle of a butterfly 45
Activity Five: Getting ready for school 46
Activity Six: My robot friend 47

Part 6: Barrier games 48

How to make a barrier board 49
Game One: Sharing shapes 50
Game Two: Barrier beads 50
Game Three: Making maps 52
Game Four: Pictures in pairs 52

Introduction

This *Speaking in Sentences* series offers a teaching resource to use with children whose lack of control over their oral language is impeding their literacy development. It is designed as an aid in implementing a programme to help individuals or groups of children as part of the whole class programme for ages 6-10, and to provide activities for use at home or at school.

In addition, although not written specifically for teaching EAL pupils, this material would be an excellent supplement to any EAL programme.

Some problems that children may be struggling with are:

- **syntax** – ie, grammar, the structure of sentences – where children omit words or have immature forms of speech, for example:
  A kid is taking off him shoes.
  Her sat down.
- **vocabulary** – the number of words that the child understands and uses – where difficulties may include using general terms, for example:
  All vehicles are referred to as *cars*.
  Big is used for *heavy, tall, high, deep, wide.*
- **semantics** – the meaning of words and the way they relate to each other
- **fluency** – the natural flow of speech – where children use hesitant speech, or overuse words such as *um* or *I don't know.*

Once the class teacher has completed the initial assessment of a child's language needs (Part 1), a parent helper or a teaching assistant could work through the activities with him or her.

Aims of this resource

To increase children's control over oral language so that they can:

- speak in full sentences
- use correct grammatical structures
- predict text in reading, thus accelerating reading progress.

See Book 4 for a suggested one-year oral language programme for ages 6-13, which draws on all four books in the *Speaking in Sentences* series.

Curriculum links

Key Stages 1–2 (Years 1–4)

Learning strand: 1. Speaking *Most children learn to:*	
	• Speak competently and creatively for different purposes and audiences, reflecting on impact and response • Explore, develop and sustain ideas through talk
Year 1	• Tell stories and describe incidents from their own experience in an audible voice • Retell stories, ordering events using story language • Interpret a text by reading aloud with some variety in pace and emphasis • Experiment with and build new stores of words to communicate in different contexts
Year 2	• Speak with clarity and use appropriate intonation when reading and reciting texts • Explain ideas and processes using imaginative and adventurous vocabulary and non-verbal gestures to support communication
Year 3	• Present information, ensuring that items are clearly sequenced, relevant details are included and accounts are ended effectively • Develop and use specific vocabulary in different contexts
Year 4	• Offer reasons and evidence for their views, considering alternative opinions • Tell stories effectively and convey detailed information coherently for listeners
Learning strand: 2. Listening and responding *Most children learn to:*	
	• Understand, recall and respond to speakers' implicit and explicit meanings
Year 1	• Listen with sustained concentration, building new stores of words in different contexts • Listen to and follow instructions accurately, asking for help and clarification if necessary
Year 2	• Listen to others in class, ask relevant questions and follow instructions • Listen to talk by an adult, remember some specific points and identify what they have learned
Year 3	• Follow up others' points and show whether they agree or disagree in whole-class discussion
Learning strand: 3. Group discussion and interaction *Most children learn to:*	
	• Participate in conversations, making appropriate contributions building on others' suggestions and responses
Year 1	• Take turns to speak, listen to others' suggestions and talk about what they are going to do • Ask and answer questions, makes relevant contributions, offer suggestions and take turns
Year 2	• Listen to each other's views and preferences
Year 3	• Actively include and respond to all members of the group
Year 4	• Take different roles in groups and use the language appropriate to them • Identify the main points of each speaker, compare their arguments and how they are presented

Source: Adapted from the Primary Framework for Literacy and Mathematics 2006

Part

Diagnostic tools

The following assessment of a child's oral language needs should be undertaken by the class teacher. The final page of this part, Assessment – summary and analysis, is a tool for making a systematic, detailed diagnosis.

Language sample

Ask your pupil to look at the picture on the next page and to tell you as much as they can about it. Use questions like:

What is happening here?
What else can you see?
Can you see anyone else on the beach?
What are they doing?
What are the people wearing?

Use a tape recorder for an accurate record of what the child says.

At the beach

Oral language sentences

Tell the child, *I am going to read out a sentence and I want you to repeat it after me.* Write the words the child says over the original sentence as if you were taking a running record in reading.

Score one mark for each sentence correctly repeated.

The child's responses will indicate the level of language they can retain and understand. If the child cannot repeat Level Two sentences accurately, they will be able to follow only very simple instructions and read very simple texts.

Your assessment may also indicate that you should adjust your classroom language.

Level One

1. Jason is riding his bike.
2. Dad is going to work.
3. Kate is playing with her bike.
4. Mum is making me a cake.
5. I can't find my book.
6. Puppy is digging a hole.
7. I've lost my book.
8. That's my new teacher.
9. My friend's brother is sick.
10. I know where you live.

/10

Level Two

1. I saw the dog eat his bone.
2. The man put his bag into the car.
3. For my birthday Mum bought me a DVD.
4. Can you come to my house?
5. The bird on the post is going to fly away.
6. My brother watched his favourite programme on TV.
7. The girl is going to swim in the pool.
8. My sister likes to play netball.
9. I hope it won't rain after school.
10. There are some big logs on that truck.

Opposites

Say to the child, *Cold is the opposite of hot. What is the opposite of …*

1. *big*
2. *good*
3. *happy*
4. *fast*
5. *quiet*

Plurals

Say to the child, *Look at this picture and tell me what you see.*

1.

2.

3.

4.

For this one you may have to ask more questions such as, *Can you think of another word to tell me what is in the picture?*

5.

6.

Vocabulary

Ask the child to name these objects.

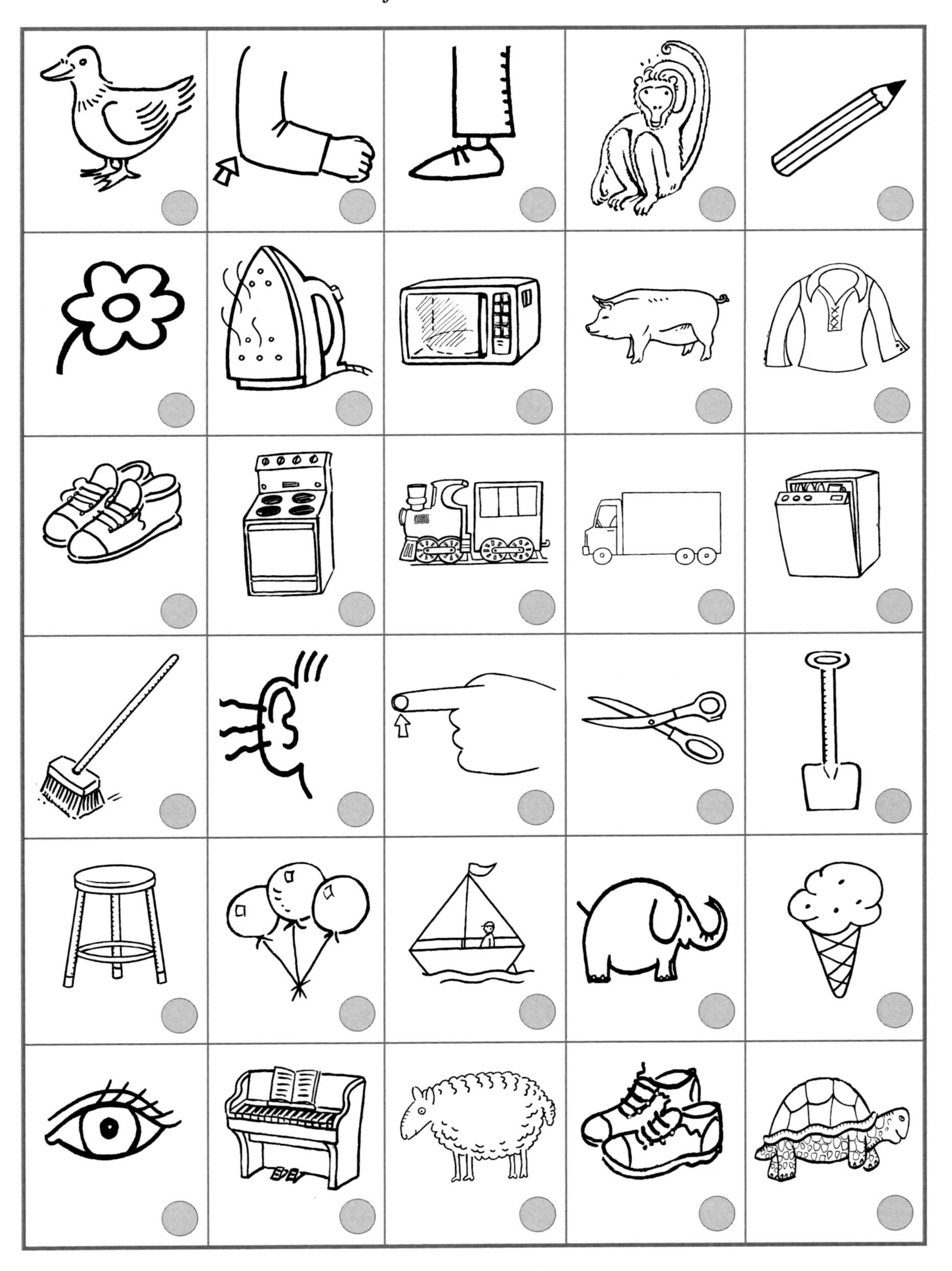

Assessment – summary and analysis

Use this assessment template to analyse the oral language needs of each child.

Language sample

Sample

Copy relevant parts of the sample here.

Specific needs

Highlight areas where help is needed.

pronouns | verbs
prepositions | tenses
identifying objects | plurals

other: ____________________

Tick the statements that apply.

- ☐ Most statements consist of one or two words.
- ☐ Child strings words together in very simple statements.
- ☐ Child often uses structures that are different from standard English.
- ☐ Complex language structures are sometimes used.

Oral language sentences

Specific needs:

Score: /20

Opposites

Specific needs:

Score: /5

Plurals

Specific needs:

Score: /6

Identifying objects

Specific needs:

Score: /30

Part

Fun, quick and handy activities

This part offers a range of 10-minute, fun activities to slot into your programme between lessons, or before or after lunch.

Impromptu speeches

Laminate the speech topics on the following pages or paste them on to card and put them in a container. Ask a child to pull out a card and then speak for one minute on the topic (as monitored by a timekeeper).

Ask the children to think of ideas to add to your collection of topics. Occasionally, also give some children a simple peer assessment sheet (see page 15) and ask them to tick each box where the speaker has done well. Report the results back to the speaker.

Robots	My favourite holiday
Helicopters	What foods should we sell at school?
Taking care of your pet	How to keep safe on the roads
How to keep safe on the school bus	
What is a good friend?	Football
Books	My favourite sport
Dogs	Are skateboards dangerous?
My favourite television programme	
My favourite DVD	Horses

What country would you like to visit and why?

Extinct animals

Safety in the playground

Space

The things I like about school are ...

Why is recycling important?

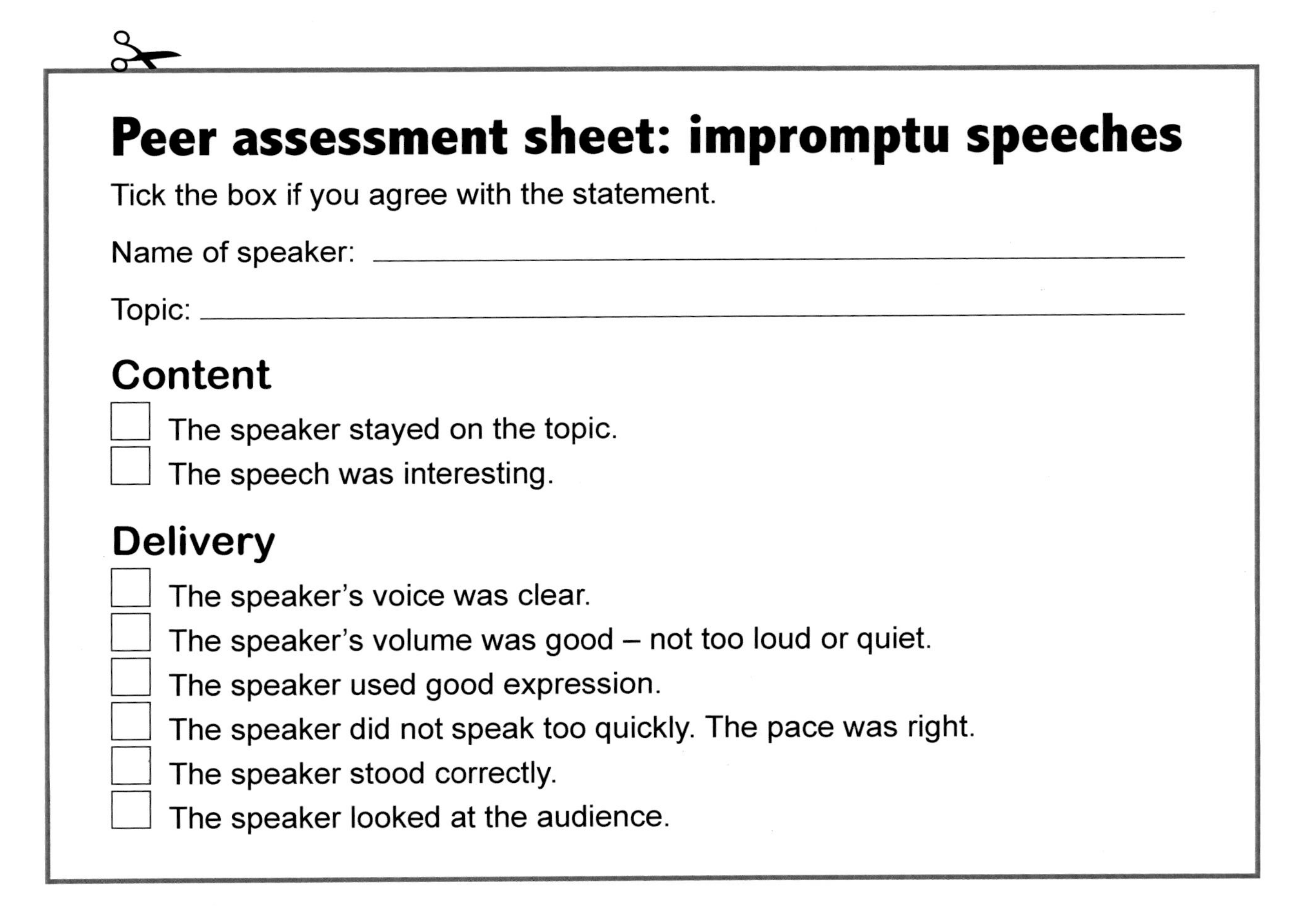

Peer assessment sheet: impromptu speeches

Tick the box if you agree with the statement.

Name of speaker: ______________________________

Topic: ______________________________

Content

- [ ] The speaker stayed on the topic.
- [ ] The speech was interesting.

Delivery

- [ ] The speaker's voice was clear.
- [ ] The speaker's volume was good – not too loud or quiet.
- [ ] The speaker used good expression.
- [ ] The speaker did not speak too quickly. The pace was right.
- [ ] The speaker stood correctly.
- [ ] The speaker looked at the audience.

Story starters

Laminate the story starters below or paste them on card and put them in a container.

For this activity, the children sit in a circle. One child holds a coloured rod, chooses a story starter from the container and starts inventing a story. When this child gets stuck, they hand the rod on to the next child, who continues with the story. This activity works well in groups of 5–6 children.

Last week when I went to the park, I saw ...
Once upon a time a spaceship landed on our school playing field ...
On the way to school this morning, I saw ...
Last night a famous visitor came to our house. We were so surprised to see ...
My dad won a million pounds and ...
The best holiday I ever had was when ...
When I was climbing up a mountain ...
Once upon a time there was a scary ...
When I leave school, I am going to ...
When the accident happened, I ...

Re-telling stories

Read a story to the children, who are seated in a circle. As a group, the children then re-tell the story. Each child says one word of the story in sequence, for example:

The – three – bears – lived ...

They continue around and around the circle in this way until the whole story has been re-told.

Telephone conversations

There are many different ways of using the telephone conversation activity. It is helpful to role-model the procedure with a pupil first.

Sit the children in pairs, back to back. Each pair pretends to have a telephone conversation. Each child takes on a particular role, such as:

- a character out of a story that has been read to the class
- a character they have invented themselves, and drawn and written about.

Each member of the pair finds out as much as they can about their partner's character.

Typical questions include:

What is your name?

Where do you live?

What sort of job do you do?

Tell me what you did today.

Extension: Have a conversation in which each member of the pair uses **only** questions.

Hide the object

One child hides an object somewhere in the room. The other children have to guess where the object is by using good questions. No one is allowed to point.

Describing in the negative

Hold up an object. Children describe the object and its attributes. Then they describe the object again, only using negatives, for example:

The scissors aren't round.

The scissors can't run.

There can be much hilarity with this activity.

Practising irregular past tense

Tell the children, *Here is a word game in which you will be talking in the past tense about things you have done.*

Drew

Give out some scraps of paper. Everyone has two minutes to draw an animal.

Two children ask the first child, *Did you draw a ...*

After two guesses, the first child says, *I drew a ...*

Fell

Push some things off the table. Ask, *What happened?*

Saw

Children go outside and look at the playground. Then they come back and sit in a circle. The first child says, *I saw a ...*

The second child has to remember what the first child saw and then add something to it: *I saw a ... and a ...* And so on ...

Caught

Throw a beanbag or ball at someone. Ask, *What did you do?*

Throw it quickly at someone else. Ask, *What did you do?*

Ran

Tell a child to go out the door and run around the field once. Ask, *What did you do?*

Expanding vocabulary – positives and negatives

Choose an object such as your hand. Look at your hand and see if you can fill the whiteboard with words that describe your hand ... dirty, smooth, veined, wrinkly.

Ask, *What can it do?* For example, grasp, pinch, tickle ...

Ask about the negatives, *What can't it do?* For example, it can't swallow ...

I spy

The age-old game of I Spy is a great way of extending oral language skills. Try it in the classroom or on a walk, looking for both the usual and the unusual.

Introducing and interviewing a speaker

Present one of the following scenarios to the children.

Your class is learning about animals in other countries. Pretend that an elephant trainer is coming to your classroom. How will you introduce him to the class? Prepare a list of questions that you can ask him too. Write some questions that will need short answers and some that will need long answers.

Your class is studying ‘People in the community who help us’. A fire fighter is coming to school to talk to you. Prepare a list of questions about a fire fighter’s job.

Pretend that one of the children or the teacher is the fire fighter. Introduce them to the class and ask them your questions.

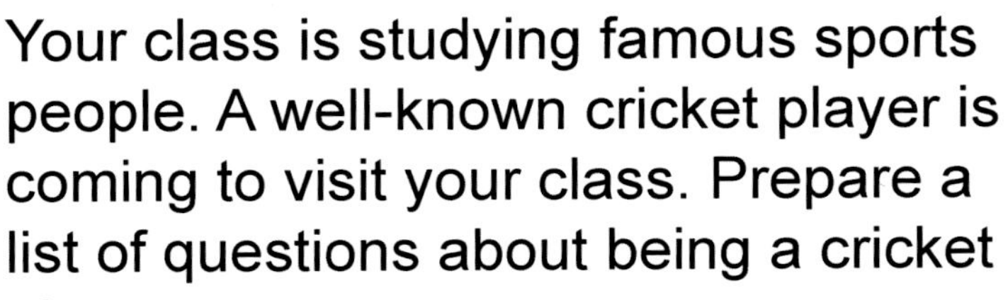

Your class is studying famous sports people. A well-known cricket player is coming to visit your class. Prepare a list of questions about being a cricket player.

Pretend that one of the children is the cricket player. Introduce them to the class and ask them your questions.

Self-access resources

Have an **oral language self-access box** in the classroom that children can use at any time. It will contain resources such as:

- pictures for the children to talk about and to write questions about (then you can read out the questions and see if the children can answer them)
- word games like Guess Who
- some sequence stories – encourage the children to talk and write about them
- paper for the children to write on
- bilingual dictionaries for your EAL pupils.

The children who are using the box need:

- to ask questions
- to guess and predict
- to try out new vocabulary
- repetition
- spoken language that links in with written language
- homework support
- tapes to take home with their reading books so that they can listen to the stories
- to learn poems and songs
- good role models.

Part

Comprehension and related activities

These activities can be used in class with an adult helper or a buddy, or can be sent home for homework. Some activities are suitable for the whole class.

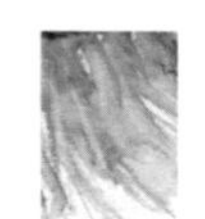

ACTIVITY ONE

The story of Pete the Pirate

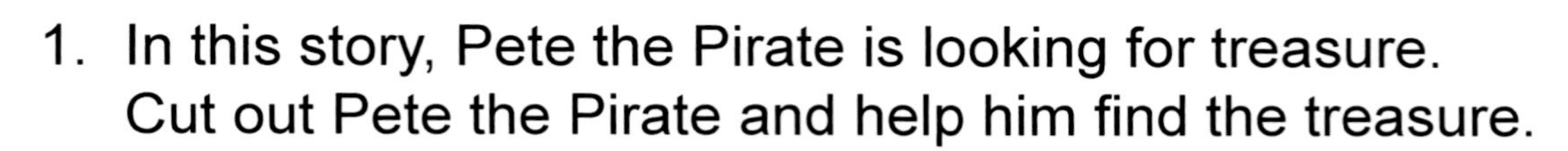

1. In this story, Pete the Pirate is looking for treasure. Cut out Pete the Pirate and help him find the treasure.
2. Read the story.

Pete dived off the sinking pirate ship.

He walked along the beach.

He kicked a shell on the sand.

He stepped over a rock.

He looked into the caves.

At the back of one of the caves he found a treasure chest.

3. Can you remember the six things that Pete did? Say the things that Pete did. Remember to use the word ending *–ed* for each thing he did.
4. Now draw the treasure.

ACTIVITY TWO

The story of the winding river

1. Read the story.

The river flowed past the oak tree and in front of the boat shed where a man was getting ready to go fishing.

It went around the flowers and past the family who were having a picnic on the grass.

It raced under the bridge and out to the sea.

2. Draw the river. You will need a blue crayon or coloured pencil.

3. Now look at the picture. Start at the beginning and say where the river went.

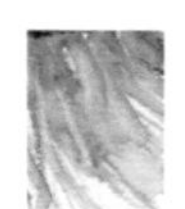

ACTIVITY THREE

The story of the horse that got away

1. Name the horse and cut it out.

   ________________ the Horse

2. Read the beginning of the story. Fill in the gaps with the name of the horse.

> Today the door of _____'s stable was left open.
>
> ______ the Horse jumped over the fence and ...

3. Now you finish the story. What did the horse do? Where did the horse go?

For Question 3

Extend your pupil by saying things like:

That's a good idea. What else could he have done? What did he do next?

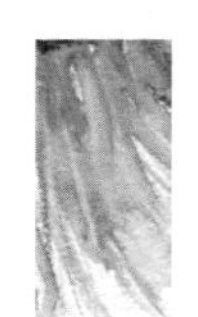

ACTIVITY FOUR

The story of the ball that rolled and rolled

1. Read the story.

Toby was playing in the garden. He kicked the ball over the fence. It bounced down the hill and across the road. It rolled under a fence and it kept on rolling. It rolled down the path, through the grass and nearly squashed a spider. It stopped beside a dog that was sleeping in the sun.

2. Now draw the rest of the picture and use arrows to show where the ball went.
3. Tell your teacher where the ball went.

ACTIVITY FIVE

The story of Samantha the Spider

1. Read the story.

> Samantha the Spider crawled in through the window.
>
> She spun a web in the corner of the window, and swung by a thread.
>
> She climbed down the wall and crawled across the carpet.
>
> She went up the back of a chair where Kate was watching TV and jumped on to Kate's nose.

2. Draw arrows to show where Samantha the spider went.
3. Now you tell the story.
   Use the words below to help you.
   The spider crawled in …
   She climbed down … and …
   The spider went …
   It jumped …
   Kate yelled …
4. Say what you think Kate did next.

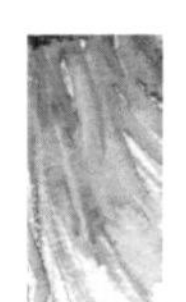

ACTIVITY SIX

The story of Andy the Astronaut

1. Read the story.

Andy the Astronaut was excited.

He was frightened.

He was nervous.

He was going to the moon.

He would travel in a spaceship
that would be launched by a powerful rocket.

Andy thought about the moon and about everything he knew about the moon.

The moon is our nearest neighbour in space.

The moon moves around the Earth. It takes one month to travel around the Earth.

The moon has no air or water.

There is very little gravity on the moon. Gravity is the force that pulls objects towards the Earth. When astronauts move around on the moon, they need to wear a heavy spacesuit. They feel light and can jump much further than they can when they are on the Earth.

There are craters on the moon. Craters are made when rocks fall on to the moon from space.

ACTIVITY SIX CONTINUED

2. Now answer the questions. Speak in complete sentences.

   (a) How did Andy feel?
   Answer: *Andy felt …*

   (b) Where was Andy going?
   Answer: *Andy was going …*

   (c) How would Andy travel to the moon?
   Answer: *He would travel in …*

   (d) Why do astronauts need to wear a heavy spacesuit on the moon?
   Answer: *Astronauts need to wear* a heavy spacesuit *on the moon because …*

   (e) Which is closer to the Earth: the moon or the sun?
   Answer: *The* ______________ *is closer to Earth.*

   (f) What is a crater?

   (g) What is gravity?

   (h) Does the moon move?

ACTIVITY SEVEN

Conversation – what would you like?

1. Read and act.

ACTIVITY EIGHT

Fill the gaps – how often?

Read each sentence to an adult or a friend. Say *usually*, *sometimes*, *often*, *never* or *always* in the space.

1. I __________________ write a letter on our computer.
2. I __________________ write a letter to my grandma.
3. I __________________ clean my teeth after breakfast.
4. I __________________ feed the cat.
5. I __________________ feed the dog.
6. I __________________ lay the table.
7. I __________________ light the fire.
8. I __________________ do my homework.
9. I __________________ go to the pictures.
10. I __________________ go to the park with my friends.
11. I __________________ go to the park with my family.
12. I __________________ bring a packed lunch to school.
13. A supermarket __________________ sells bread.

ACTIVITY EIGHT CONTINUED

14. A butcher ______________ sells sausages.

15. You can ______________ buy paint at a supermarket.

16. You can ______________ buy apples at a butcher.

17. You can ______________ buy bananas at a flower shop.

18. I ______________ ride on a bike.

19. I ______________ ride on a tractor.

20. I ______________ ride on a bus.

21. I ______________ ride in a car.

22. I ______________ ride in a taxi.

23. I ______________ sail in a boat.

24. My family ______________ eats fish.

25. My family ______________ eats tomatoes.

26. My family ______________ eats lamb.

27. My family ______________ eats lettuce.

28. My family ______________ eats burgers.

29. I ______________ make my bed.

30. My friends ______________ care about me.

Part

Using pronouns

Use these activities to help the children use pronouns correctly. They focus particularly on third person pronouns (*he, she, they* etc) but could be adapted to reinforce the other pronouns as well.

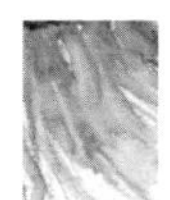

ACTIVITY ONE

Action book

Children make an action book at home or at school.
They cut pictures from the newspaper or magazines and talk about what the people are doing. Then they write what the people are doing under the pictures using *he*, *she* and *they*. For example:

She is throwing the ball.

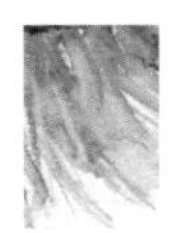

ACTIVITY TWO

He and *she* card game

1. Copy the pictures (Sets One and Two on the following pages) on to card and cut them out individually.
2. A small group of children sit in a circle. The cards are in a pile, face down in the middle of the circle.
3. A child picks up a card and looks at the picture without letting the other children see it. The child mimes the action on the card.
4. The other children say what the child is doing, using a pronoun and a full sentence. For example,

   She is running or *He is winking*.

Set One

Copy these pictures on to card and cut out each one.

Set Two

Copy these pictures on to card and cut out each one.

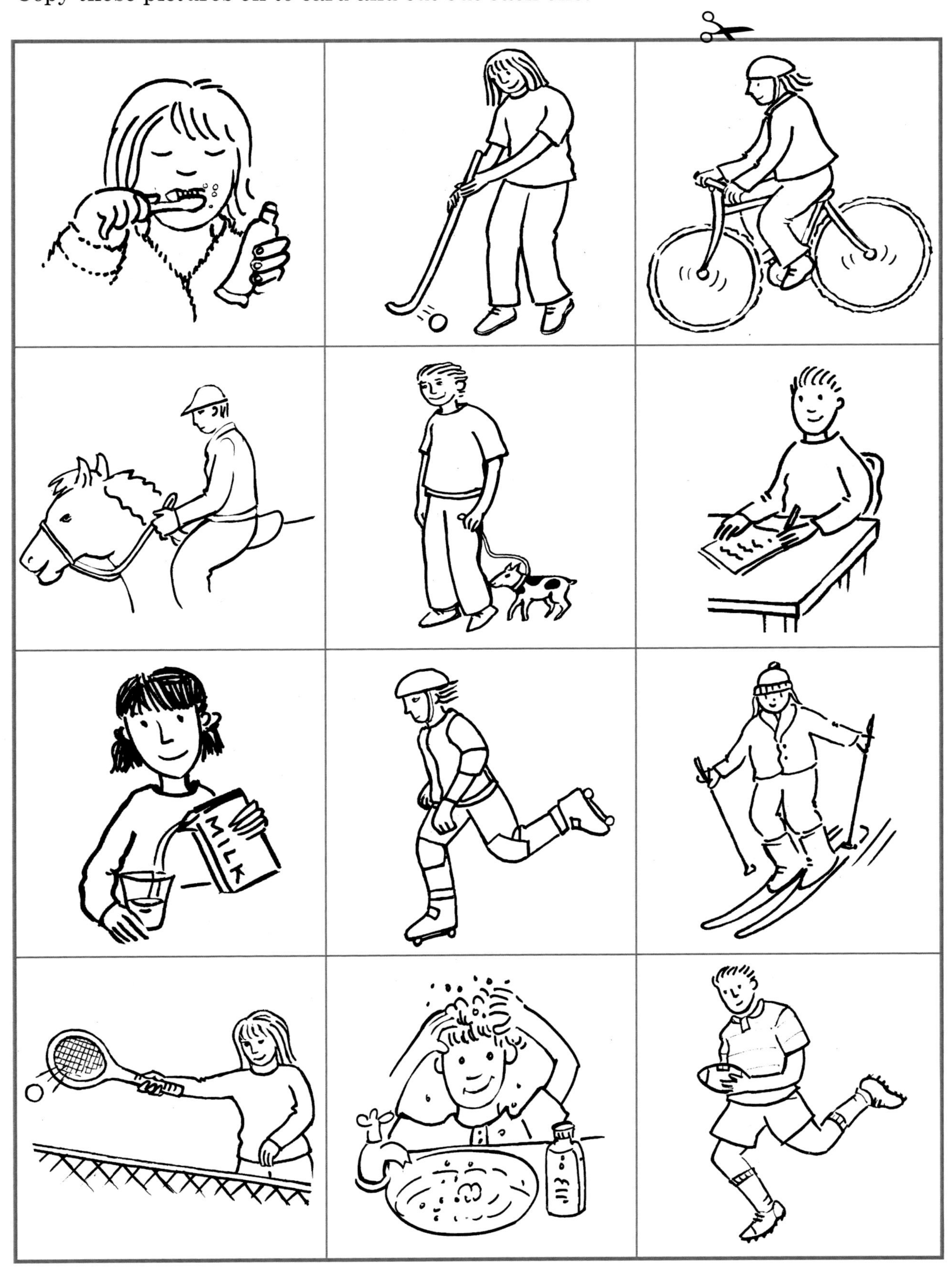

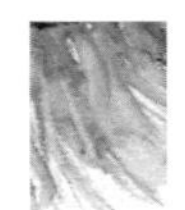

ACTIVITY THREE

He and *she* action pictures

Say what the people are doing. Use *he* or *she*. Then write what they are doing under the pictures.

He is … She is …

ACTIVITY FOUR

He, ***she***, ***it*** and ***they*** action pictures

Say what the people and the animals are doing. Use *he*, *she*, *it* or *they*. Then write what they are doing under the pictures.

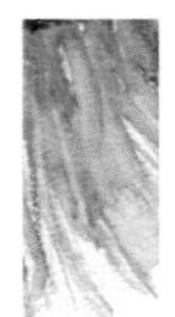

ACTIVITY FIVE

Sentence completion with *his*, *her* and *their*

Say each sentence out loud. Finish the sentence by saying *his*, *her* or *their* in the space. Then write the correct word in the space.

1. James is reading ______________ book.
2. Peter is driving ______________ tractor.
3. Jason is looking at ______________ watch.
4. Paul is tidying ______________ room.
5. Amanda is making ______________ bed.
6. Anna is reading ______________ book.
7. Erin is writing a letter to ______________ friend.
8. William and Jack are riding ______________ bikes.
9. The girls are playing with ______________ dolls.
10. Hannah and Mark are putting ______________

    lunches in ______________ bags.
11. Erin was picking some flowers to put in

    ______________ bedroom.
12. Dad parked ______________ car in the garage.

ACTIVITY SIX

Story completion with *his*, *her* and *they*

Read the story aloud. Finish the story by saying *his* or *her* or *they* in each space. Then write the correct words in the spaces.

Mum, Dad, Jack and Amanda are going on holiday to the beach. ____________ will be staying in a house near the beach and ____________ will be able to walk to the beach each day to swim and play on the beach. Mum has packed a large sun umbrella, a beach towel for each person and some sunscreen lotion so that ____________ won't get sunburnt. She has also packed ____________ shorts, T-shirts and swimming costumes. Dad has put two chairs into the car. One is for Mum and the other is for him to sit on while ____________ are at the beach.

What has Amanda put into her suitcase? She has put in ____________ Barbie doll and all Barbie's clothes. She has packed ____________ bucket and spade and ____________ favourite books. Soon there will be no room for ____________ clothes.

Jack is making a pile of things that he wants to take on holiday. He has ____________ snorkelling gear and ____________ surfboard. He wants to take ____________ new camera. There is no television in the beach house so he can't take ____________ DVDs. Don't forget your clothes, Jack!

ACTIVITY SEVEN

Conversation – what can you see?

1. Point to the picture and say:

   Can you see a mouse?
   Yes, I can see it.

   Can you see a teacher?
   Yes, I can see her.

   Can you see three flowers?
   No, I can't see them.

   Can you see a policeman?
   No, I can't see him.

   Can you see …

three fish	a donkey
a computer	a skateboard
a monster	a telephone
a rocket	a policewoman
two books	an alien
a nurse	a camera

Part 5

Sequence stories

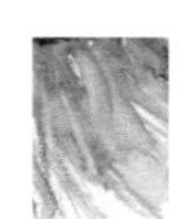

ACTIVITY ONE

Andy the Astronaut's space trip

1. Cut out the pictures.
2. Can you put the pictures in the correct order?
3. Say what Andy did this week.
4. Write what he did on the lines.

ACTIVITY TWO

Building a story from pictures

Cut out the pictures and arrange them in the correct order. Talk about what is happening in each picture. Then write the story on the lines under the picture or in your book.

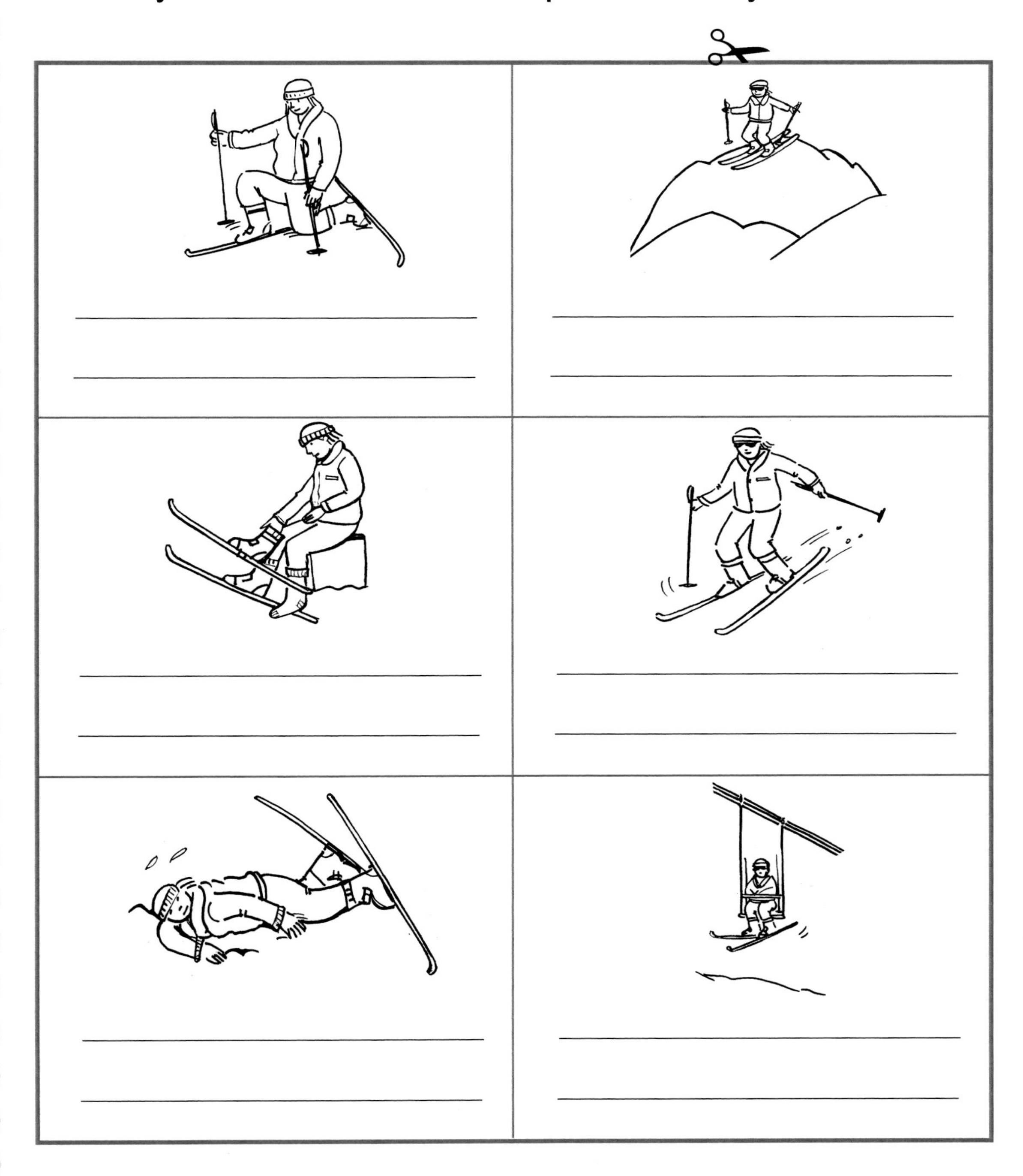

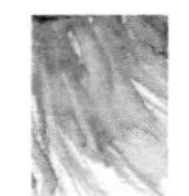

ACTIVITY THREE

The life cycle of a frog

Cut out the pictures and arrange them in the correct order. Talk about what is happening in each picture. Then write the story on the lines under the picture or in your book.

ACTIVITY FOUR

The life cycle of a butterfly

Cut out the pictures and arrange them in the correct order. Talk about what is happening in each picture. Then write the story on the lines under the picture or in your book.

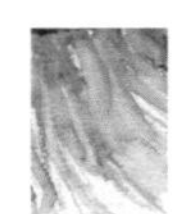

ACTIVITY FIVE

Getting ready for school

Cut out the pictures and arrange them in the correct order. Talk about what is happening in each picture. Then write the story on the lines under the picture or in your book.

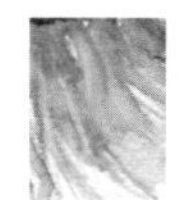

ACTIVITY SIX

My robot friend

Cut out the pictures and arrange them in the correct order. Talk about what is happening in each picture. Then write the story on the lines under the picture or in your book.

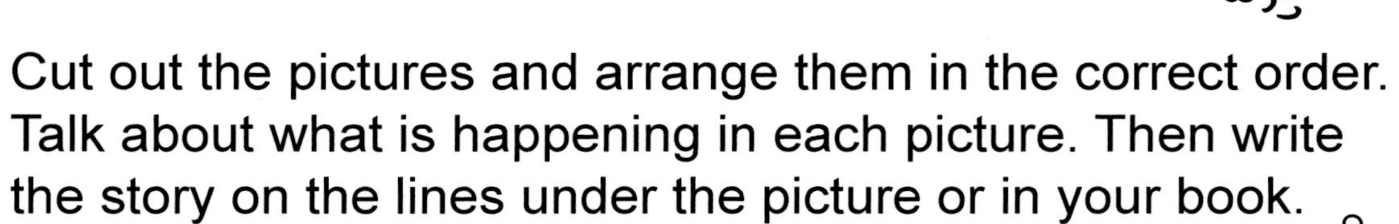

Part

Barrier games

Barrier games are great for teaching children to give clear instructions and to follow instructions. In these games, children need to use precise language and they learn to use positional vocabulary well.

Children play in pairs. For each game you will need some sort of barrier so that one child can't see what the other child is doing. A suitable barrier may be as simple as a book standing upright, or getting the children to sit back to back.

Some teachers make wooden stands as barrier boards (see the next page). Once the children have painted them, you will have a class set.

How to make a barrier board

Materials

For each barrier board you will need:

- 1600 mm of 20 mm × 10 mm untreated wood
- a 400 mm × 360 mm sheet of 3 mm MDF
- a 100 mm × 100 mm piece of 3 mm MDF.

To make the barrier boards you will also need:

- some 20 mm nails
- PVA woodworkers glue
- a set square
- a dust mask
- a hammer
- a saw.

Procedure

1. Cut the 20 mm × 10 mm wood into four 400 mm length pieces. Glue and nail these four pieces into a square (Figure 1).

   Note that the two side lengths are **on top** of the top and bottom lengths.

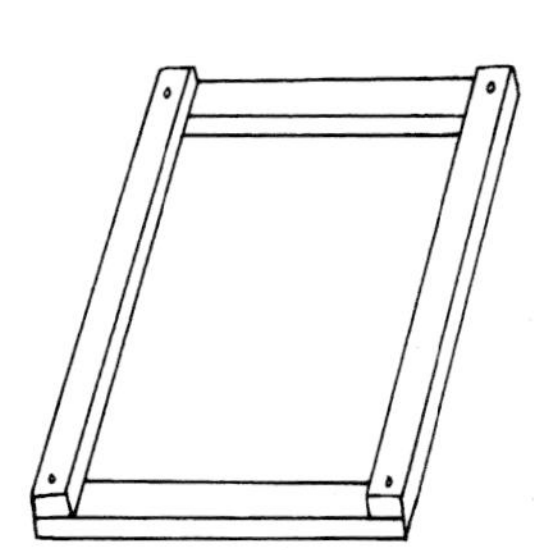

Figure 1

2. Place your 400 × 360 mm sheet of MDF inside the two side pieces so that it completely covers the middle of the square (Figure 2).

   Glue and nail along the top and bottom.

Figure 2

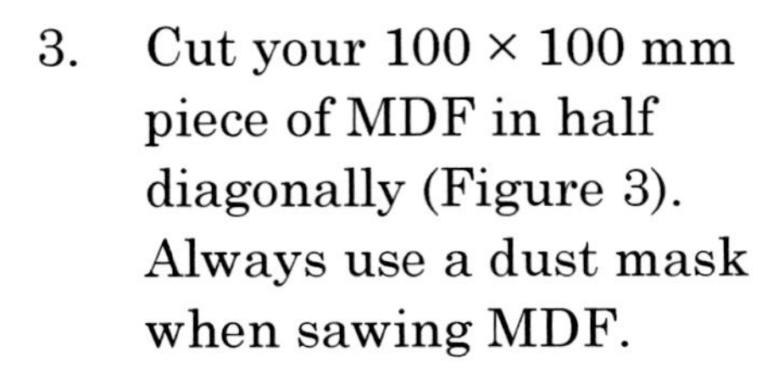

3. Cut your 100 × 100 mm piece of MDF in half diagonally (Figure 3). Always use a dust mask when sawing MDF.

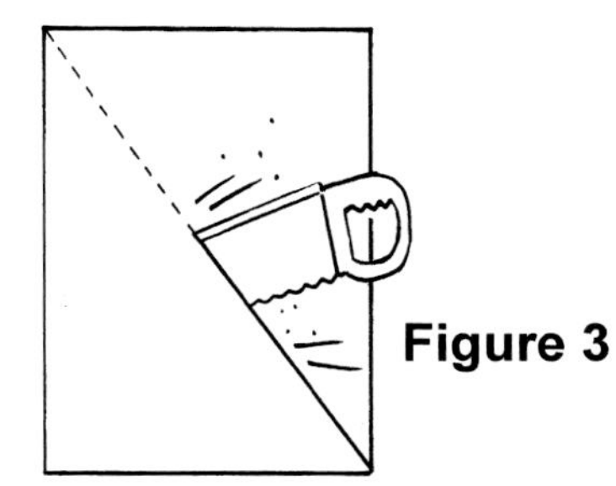

Figure 3

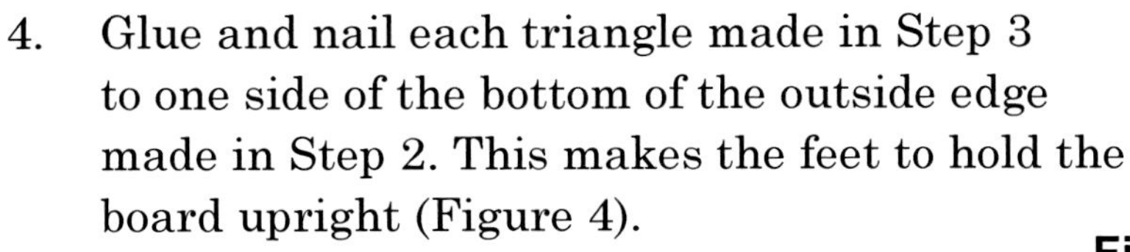

4. Glue and nail each triangle made in Step 3 to one side of the bottom of the outside edge made in Step 2. This makes the feet to hold the board upright (Figure 4).

Figure 4

You have now completed your barrier board.

GAME ONE

Sharing shapes

Materials

Each child will need:

- a set of attribute shapes (identical to their partner's set)
- a game board (see the following page).

Procedure

1. One child gives the instructions, such as:
   Put a small red triangle in the middle square in the top row.
   Put a yellow circle in the bottom corner nearest to the door.
2. Both children follow these instructions on their own board.
3. When the board is filled, or after a set time, the children see if they have made the same picture.
4. Children reverse roles and the other child gives the instructions.

GAME TWO

Barrier beads

Materials

Each child will need:

- string
- a set of threading beads.

Procedure

1. One child gives the instructions, such as:
   Put two red beads on the string and then two yellow ones.
2. Both children follow these instructions with their own beads.
3. After a set time they see if they have made the same pattern.
4. Children reverse roles and the other child gives the instructions.

Game board

Make two copies of this board and laminate each one so that they can be used over and over again.

GAME THREE
Making maps

Materials

Each pair will need:

- a local road map or a map of the school
- pencils or pens.

Procedure

1. One child instructs their partner to draw vehicles or people in appropriate places on the map. Instructions may include adding other items, such as:
   Place a rubbish bin in front of the library.
   Draw a stop sign at the corner of ... and ...
2. Children reverse roles and the other child gives the instructions.

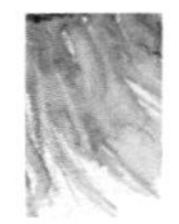

GAME FOUR
Pictures in pairs

Materials

Each child will need:

- crayons or coloured pencils
- a copy of one of the pictures on the following pages (farm, house, tropics, ocean).

Procedure

1. One child gives instructions, such as:
   Colour the bedspread red and the pillow blue.
   Colour the farmer's hat green.
   Colour the bubbles in the sea red.
2. Both children follow these instructions with their own picture.
3. After a set time, the children compare pictures to see if they are the same.
4. The children change roles and the other child gives the instructions.

WOOL